Sports Illustrated KIDS

Traditions and Superstitions

BASKETBALL'S Best TRADITIONS and WEIRDEST SUPERSTITIONS

by Elliott Smith

CAPSTONE PRESS
a capstone imprint

Published by Capstone Press, an imprint of Capstone
1710 Roe Crest Drive, North Mankato, Minnesota 56003
capstonepub.com

Library of Congress Cataloging-in-Publication Data
Names: Smith, Elliott, 1976- author.
Title: Basketball's best traditions and weirdest superstitions / by Elliott Smith.
Description: North Mankato, Minnesota : Capstone Press, 2023. | Series: Sports illustrated kids. Traditions and superstitions | Includes bibliographical references and index. | Audience: Ages 8-11 | Audience: Grades 4-6 | Summary: "Going to a basketball game? Give Elena Delle Donne a few extra seconds to say a few words before her free throw. And watch out for toilet paper at John Brown University's first home game. But first, take time out to learn the ins and outs of good fun and good luck in basketball. With engaging text and striking photos, this book will delight young sports fan with some of the best and weirdest practices on the court and in the stands"-- Provided by publisher.
Identifiers: LCCN 2022013042 (print) | LCCN 2022013043 (ebook) |
ISBN 9781666346770 (hardcover) | ISBN 9781666346787 (pdf) |
ISBN 9781666346800 (kindle edition)
Subjects: LCSH: Basketball--Miscellanea--Juvenile literature. | Superstition--Juvenile literature.
Classification: LCC GV885.1 .S59 2023 (print) | LCC GV885.1 (ebook) | DDC 796.323--dc23/eng/20220509
LC record available at https://lccn.loc.gov/2022013042
LC ebook record available at https://lccn.loc.gov/2022013043

Editorial Credits
Editor: Ericka Smith; Designer: Tracy Davies; Media Researcher: Svetlana Zhurkin; Production Specialist: Katy LaVigne

Image Credits
Alamy: Reuters/Stephen Lam, 13; Associated Press: Cal Sport Media/Ron Waite, 17, Charmin/Gareth Patterson, 27 (top), David Goldman, cover (bottom right), 16, File/Eric Gay, 11 (left), Nuccio DiNuzzo, 19; Getty Images: © NBAE/Logan Riely, 11 (right); Newscom: EFE/Craig Lassig, 23, Icon Sportswire/Julian Avram, 29, Icon Sportswire/Paul Williams, 9 (top), Icon Sportswire/William Purnell, 27 (bottom); Shutterstock: DGIM studio (burst background), cover and throughout, Eakkapon Sriharun, cover (top left and far right), Eugene Powers, 10, magicoven, 8, Mega Pixel, 6, Michael Kraus, cover (top right), Mike Flippo, 14, Monkey Business Images, 5, Mott Jordan, cover (title fonts), niwat chaiyawoot (basketball), cover and throughout, P Maxwell Photography, 20, son Photo, cover (bottom left), 26, vinap, cover (showerhead); Sports Illustrated: Andy Hayt, 15, Damian Strohmeyer, 21, David E. Klutho, 25, Erick W. Rasco, 4, 7, John W. McDonough, 9 (bottom)

All internet sites appearing in back matter were available and accurate when this book was sent to press.

Direct Quotation
Page 20, from March 24, 2021, YouTube video, Not a Sports Show, "Fact or Fiction with 'The Truth' Paul Pierce," youtube.com

Printed and bound in the USA. PO 5994

TABLE OF CONTENTS

Words in **bold** are in the glossary.

INTRODUCTION

HOOP DREAMS

People all over the world love to play and watch basketball. The hustle on the court easily keeps the players on their toes. It can keep the fans on their feet too!

Everyone brings their own unique traditions and superstitions to the game. They make the game more exciting. One player might wear a special pair of shoes. Another might have a favorite spot on the court. And fans might have a cool way to celebrate their team's success on the court.

Whether practiced in a small school gym or a huge arena, traditions and superstitions are a major part of what makes basketball fun.

CHAPTER 1

PREGAME RITUALS

Before the game begins, there's plenty happening behind the scenes. To get ready for a big game, some National Basketball Association (NBA) players follow **strict** routines. Keeping everything in order helps them focus on the job ahead.

NAP TIME

Giannis Antetokounmpo is one of the NBA's best players. The Milwaukee Bucks forward won the league's Most Valuable Player (MVP) award in 2019 and 2020. What's his secret? A pregame nap. Antetokounmpo takes a nearly three-hour nap before every game.

The superstar started this habit as a teenager in Greece. His father insisted he sleep before games. At first, Antetokounmpo didn't like it. Now, it's a key part of his pregame routine.

A SPECIAL DRINK

Women's National Basketball Association (WNBA) veteran Sue Bird has been in the league for 18 seasons. Over the years, she's developed a locked-in set of pregame routines.

One of her most unique habits happens on her way to the arena. Bird drinks one cup of coffee 90 minutes before the game. That may sound weird, but coffee provides a boost to the brain and the body.

No one can argue with her results. The point guard is the WNBA's all-time leader in number of games played. And she has the most **assists**.

Bird (right) in a game against the Connecticut Sun in 2015

EARLY BIRD

Hall of Famer Ray Allen was serious about his warm-ups. He was often the first player on the court. He would start shooting at 4:30 p.m. for a 7:00 p.m. game.

FASHION FORWARD

The pregame walk from the bus to the locker room was once a small part of a player's day. Recently, it's turned into a red-carpet entrance.

NBA and WNBA players use this walk to show off their fashion sense. Some players have worn jaw-dropping outfits.

Russell Westbrook and Tamera "Ty" Young are among basketball's biggest fashion stars. Whether in ripped denim or sharp suits, they know how to make a statement.

CLEAN FREAK

There's clean and there's Rajon Rondo clean. The Cleveland Cavaliers point guard takes as many as five showers before a game! He says he does his best thinking in the water.

Westbrook arriving for a playoff game in San Antonio in 2016

Young arriving to play for the Las Vegas Aces in 2019

CHAPTER 2

ON-COURT QUIRKS

The action on the court is fast and furious. Fast breaks, long shots, and bold **blocks** are huge plays that build excitement. But there are plenty of small actions that make a difference too. Look closely and you'll see some of the best players doing some interesting things.

CHEW ON THIS

Stephen Curry of the Golden State Warriors is one of the greatest shooters of all time. He also has a bad habit that helps him concentrate. He chews constantly on his mouth guard. At the free throw line, he'll often flip it outside of his mouth.

In one season, Curry will go through about 12 mouth guards. He admits the habit is a little gross. But it helps him play better.

Fans think this practice is worth it too. In 2016, one of Curry's used mouth guards sold at **auction** for $3,190!

SUPER SHORTS

The best NBA players don't need any superstitions, right? Wrong. Michael Jordan had many quirks during his long career.

Jordan's most famous superstition started during his days at the University of North Carolina (UNC). He had a pair of Tar Heels shorts that he considered lucky. When he came to the NBA to play for the Chicago Bulls, he continued wearing them. The UNC shorts would often peek out under his Bulls shorts. So Jordan started wearing longer shorts.

Jordan continued to wear his UNC shorts throughout his career. And he started the trend of NBA players wearing longer shorts.

A young Michael Jordan attempting a dunk in 1987

WINNING ROUTINE

Elena Delle Donne is the best free throw shooter in the history of basketball. By the end of the 2021 season, the Washington Mystics forward had made 93.9 percent of her free throws!

Her success is due to a carefully followed routine. During practice, she works on free throws and must make 10 shots in a row. During a game, she dribbles three times, says a few words to herself, and shoots. She's been practicing this routine since eighth grade. It helps her feel confident.

SHOE TALK

Many players have started writing messages on their sneakers for inspiration. And putting the names of friends and family on their shoes is considered good luck. On LeBron James's shoes, you'll find the names or nicknames of members of his family. Kyrie Irving adds *Whiplash*, the title of a film he discovered through Kobe Bryant. It encourages him to keep pushing himself to play well.

SPALDING
verizon

CHAPTER 3

TEAM TRADITIONS

It's not just individual players who have traditions. Sometimes an entire team will come together to help get a win. Even if a player isn't superstitious, being a good teammate sometimes means joining in anyway.

LOTTERY LUCK

The lottery is a chance for teams to land a top pick in the NBA Draft. The worst teams in the league are assigned combinations of four numbers. Then, they mix up ping-pong balls with numbers and select four balls. The team with that combination receives the first draft pick. They repeat the process to select the next three picks.

Teams use good luck charms to try to earn one of the top selections. Some use former players as their representatives during the lottery. Others bring **trinkets** from their children or fans.

Once, former Orlando Magic general manager Pat Williams brought a box of Lucky Charms to the lottery. Another time, a former Philadelphia 76ers owner used a crystal ball from Ireland as his good luck charm.

PB&J EVERY DAY

In 2007, the Boston Celtics had a great team. But something was missing. It was peanut butter and jelly sandwiches!

One night, team leader Kevin Garnett ate a pregame sandwich—a peanut butter and jelly sandwich. The team played well during that game. From that point on, Garnett demanded the team eat peanut butter and jelly sandwiches before every game. The Celtics won the NBA Championship that year.

"Who didn't like peanut butter and jelly growing up?" the Celtics' Paul Pierce said. "So everybody just gravitated to it. It'd just be a row of peanut butter and jelly sandwiches."

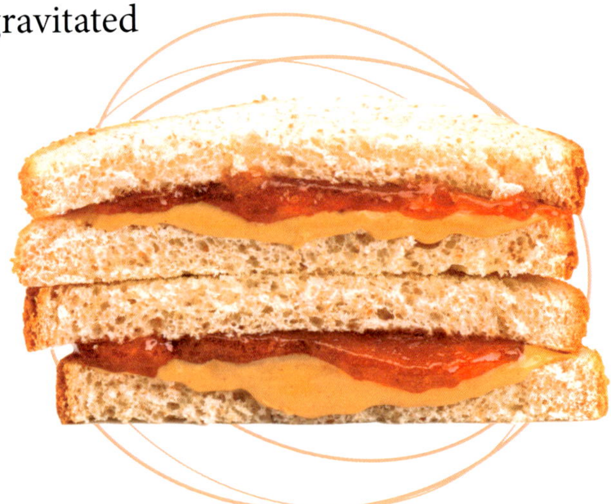

Garnett takes a shot during a Celtics game against the Toronto Raptors in 2007.

NO TIPS

During the 2016 and 2017 seasons, the Minnesota Lynx did something strange. They would try not to win the opening tip of the game. Sometimes they would make fake jumps as the referee threw the ball up. If the tip came toward a Lynx player, she would back up.

The team refused to say whether this was on purpose. But at one point, they had lost more than 30 straight opening tips. And no one on the team would talk about it.

Some think it could be a strategy. The team was making sure they got the ball at the start of the second and third quarters—for a boost later in the game.

MAYO CLINIC
3
verizon
MAYO CLINIC
21
55

CHAPTER 4

ARENA TRADITIONS

Going to a basketball game should be fun. That's why fans and teams have created traditions that make the off-court action exciting. From T-shirt cannons to amazing halftime shows, these practices help keep fans coming back.

MASCOT MANIA!

No mascot in sports works harder than the Hawk of St. Joseph's University. At the start of the game, the Hawk starts flapping its wings. It doesn't stop until the game is over—not even at halftime.

The Phoenix Suns' Gorilla is one of the NBA's most unique mascots. How did a dunking gorilla come to represent the Suns? In 1980, a messenger from a singing telegram service came to a game. The messenger was dressed as a gorilla. The team's security suggested he do some dancing during a time-out. The fans loved it. So the gorilla kept coming back. And he's been part of the team ever since.

SILENT NIGHT shhh!

It may seem weird not to cheer when a team scores. But for the students at Taylor University, it's a holiday tradition. The last men's game just before Christmas is the school's Silent Night game. Students dress up and stay silent until the team scores its tenth point. Then everyone goes crazy.

TP TOSS

Throwing objects onto the court earns a team a technical foul. But at John Brown University, that is a cherished tradition.

Starting in 1984, John Brown fans began bringing toilet paper to the first home game of the season. When the team scores its first basket, fans throw the rolls onto the court. The event is so popular that fans throw more than 2,000 rolls of toilet paper onto the court.

Even though it's a tradition, John Brown earns an automatic technical foul every year.

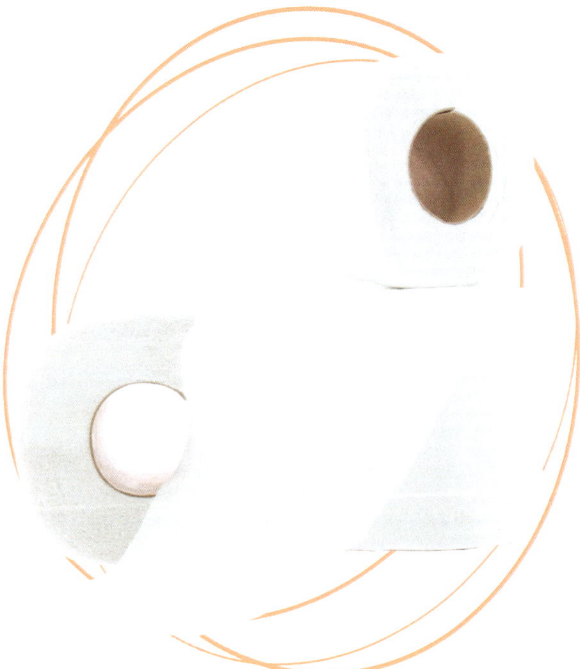

Students throw toilet paper during John Brown University's first home basketball game of 2015.

AN OLD CHANT

At the University of Kansas, students chant "Rock chalk, Jayhawk, KU" just before a game begins. This slow chant, called the "Rock Chalk Chant," dates back to 1886, when it started as a cheer created for a science club on campus.

INSIDE OUTSIDE

The biggest games of the season—the playoffs—draw the largest crowds to an arena. Sometimes that happens even when teams are on the road!

When their team is away from home, fans have started watching playoff games outside the arena. Large crowds show up. And they cheer their teams on in front of huge video boards.

More than 10,000 fans showed up to watch the Toronto Raptors' playoff run in 2019. The area where fans gathered became known as Jurassic Park. The same thing happened in Milwaukee's Deer District when the Bucks won the championship in 2021.

Raptors fans watch their team play the Warriors in Oakland in 2019.

GLOSSARY

assist (uh-SIST)—a pass that leads to a score by a teammate

auction (AWK-shuhn)—a sale during which items are sold to the person who offers the most money

block (BLOK)—when a defender knocks a shot away from the basket

strict (STRIKT)—sticking to a particular set of rules

trinket (TRIN-kit)—a small, cheap object

READ MORE

Jordan, James H. *Unbelievable Stories of Michael Jordan*. Sheridan, WY: Kids Castle Press, 2021.

Kelley, K. C. *WNBA Young Stars*. Mankato, MN: Child's World, 2020.

Levit, Joe. *Meet Stephen Curry*. Minneapolis: Lerner, 2023.

INTERNET SITES

Jr. NBA
jr.nba.com

Kiddle: National Basketball Association Facts for Kids
kids.kiddle.co/National_Basketball_Association

Kidzworld: March Madness Fun Facts
kidzworld.com/article/31414-march-madness-fun-facts

INDEX

ABOUT THE AUTHOR

Elliott Smith is a freelance writer, editor, and author. He has covered a wide variety of subjects, including sports, entertainment, and travel, for newspapers, magazines, and websites. He has written a nonfiction book about the Washington Nationals and a children's book about Bryce Harper. He lives in the Washington, DC, area with his wife and two children.